Healing with Fasting

REFLECTIONS ON THE HOLY MONTH OF RAMADAN

Craig Considine - Farah Dualeh - Enes Kanter Freedom - M. Fethullah Gülen - Sana Khan
Allen S. Maller - Hannah Matus - Justin Pahl - Brandon Richey
Kathleen St.Onge - Martha Trunk - Hakan Yesilova

Published by Tughra Books
www.tughrabooks.com
335 Clifton Ave. Clifton New Jersey 07011

Contents

HEALING WITH FASTING

Ramadan is the most blissful time for Muslims. As you will be reading in the following pages, it is a full month of spiritual retreat dedicated to worship, fasting, and charity. Families and friends reunite to break bread together and join in prayers. Ramadan is like Thanksgiving celebrated for a month.

More recently, Ramadan meals have started to serve a new purpose, that of promoting interfaith and intercultural dialogue. Muslim citizens living in non-Muslim societies have taken the advice of the Prophet to serve one's neighbor and share meals with them. In this way, Ramadan iftar meals bring together people from different traditions and all walks of life to learn from one another and enjoy new friendships. This booklet covers this most significant Islamic month from various aspects and how it influences personal lives.

"Fasting is a shield ..."

VIGILANCE
WITH FASTING

by Kathleen St.Onge

A common western tradition is the "New Year's resolution, in which one vows to exercise self-control over a specific weakness such as candy or smoking. Commitment to Ramadan rises from a similar foundation of self-control in a much more disciplined way and the primary intention of observance should be the pleasure of God only. The glorious Qur'an prescribes fasting for us so that we may learn "self-restraint." The miracle is that self-restraint is about much more than skipping lunch. Continual, practiced self-restraint is at the very root of one of the key attributes of a believer: vigilance.

What is vigilance?

Vigilance is the condition of watchfulness and guardedness that acts as a personal warning system to keep us away from anything that can weaken our faith. By the grace of God, we have been sent clear signs of how erosion can slowly change even the hardest substances on earth. Rocks stronger than any human can slowly deteriorate, one handful of sand at a time, through the gradual action of natural forces like water and wind... until a shoreline completely changes. The melting of glaciers is another sign for us—by the slightest shift in the earth's temperature, the ice starts to melt away, eventually changing the geography of the entire world.

In human lives, erosion happens in the social sphere, when we slowly compromise our values and our beliefs. A Muslim boy from my son's school told him last week that it was not necessary to wash before prayers—only preferable. Perhaps next, the idea may creep in that one or more of the daily prayers is not necessary, only preferable. Unless we clearly hold to our boundaries, they will recede naturally as time passes. The signs are all around us.

We are all at risk from this kind of erosion. No man or woman wakes up one morning and thinks, "I will ruin my family today." It begins slowly with just an improper glance or the breath of a fragrance, and temptation is born. And no teen ever thinks, "I will become an alcoholic." Rather, it starts with just "one sip" from a friend's drink or one party "because a friend is going." And what of the male or female believers who work under tough business conditions? Day after day, people are getting busier with heavy schedules and prayer times can't always be accommodated. After years of this, how strong will belief—or practice—be? Clearly, as soon as vigilance is weak, erosion sets in. How else can we explain how millions of people around the world today commit "forgotten" prohibitions?

Are any of us strong enough to resist this kind of slipping? How many of us flip channels on the television and settle on shows we know are inappropriate if only for a minute. Inappropriate topics and images fill our senses and are hard to "shake" once they set themselves on our retinas and eardrums. So instead of having the scriptures in our

... AND OUR TIME IS SLOWLY ERODED— TIME WHICH IS SO PRECIOUS, EVERY SECOND A GIFT, AND MAYBE THE LAST.

heads as we drive from A to B, we are humming the top 10. And how simple it is for our children to copy the entertainers who mock everyone just for a laugh! How easily we—and our families—begin to attend to marketing ploys which aim to make us yearn for the "ornaments" of this life. In such a way, our thoughts are slowly replaced by useless ramblings and distractions, and our time is slowly eroded—time which is so precious, every second a gift, and maybe the last.

For communities and nations, vigilance is an even bigger challenge. Our voices are often quiet on important issues which will affect humanity forever. We are usually busy struggling with our own existence, and it is hard to challenge the status quo. In fact, there is so much we don't know that it becomes very complex to guard ourselves and remain vigilant. Guarding faith takes constant effort—but recovering a lost faith is even harder.

In essence, vigilance is really about developing and guarding personal boundaries. Through Ramadan, we learn to recognize our bodies as "gates" through which we can allow or prevent the passage of anything. We all know the feeling that follows the fast everyday—each time we put something in our mouths after sundown, we can't help but quickly ask ourselves if it is ok to do so. This reflex is the key operating mechanism for vigilance. Each time something comes to any of our senses, we should question if it is good for us or not. If we do this each and every time, we will be safe and we will be in God's favor, as this is His clear promise to us. If we remain watchful over ourselves, God will keep watch over us.

> **VIGILANCE IS REALLY ABOUT DEVELOPING AND GUARDING PERSONAL BOUNDARIES. THROUGH RAMADAN, WE LEARN TO RECOGNIZE OUR BODIES AS "GATES" THROUGH WHICH WE CAN ALLOW OR PREVENT THE PASSAGE OF ANYTHING.**

Kathleen St.Onge is the author of *Bridge to Light*: *Spiritual Wayfaring Towards Islam.*

SHARING
WITH FASTING

by Justin Pahl

When I think about Ramadan in Istanbul, I first think about bread. More specifically, I think about Ramazan pide.

At first blush, Ramazan pide is simple. It's a round flat bread, the puffy top latticed like a checkerboard and dressed with sesame seeds. Though it's available year-round, it was easiest to find during Ramadan when, as sunset drew near, bakeries churned out loaf after loaf, selling it wrapped in paper and still warm.

I discovered Ramazan pide my first Ramadan, and my first summer, in Istanbul. It was July 2013, a hot, humid month. I'd been in Istanbul four months by then, and was still completely enamored of the city—its thoughtful people, its layers of history. I wanted to drink all of it in.

I was particularly fascinated by the way Islam was interwoven with Turkish culture. As an American Lutheran, I knew very little about Islam beyond the American right's demonization of the faith. What I saw firsthand in Istanbul was a living, nuanced faith—one that inspired discipline (and yes, occasionally dogma) but also kindness. Islam, like the other monotheistic faiths, encourages watching out for one's neighbor, and I felt that acutely wherever in the city I wandered (and I wandered a lot of places). Wherever I found myself, there was always someone willing to offer directions, a smile, or a cup of bitter Turkish tea—and this generosity of spirit is at the heart of Islam.

This generosity was especially prevalent during Ramadan. Though I wasn't fasting like many of my colleagues and friends—

and though I wasn't a practicing Muslim—I was often invited to iftar, or fast-breaking, meals. I was welcomed into my friends' and co-workers' homes and treated like family. I relished the first bite of date, the traditional way of breaking the fast, as well as the heaps of extraordinary food that followed. But mostly, I enjoyed the kindness and camaraderie of my companions, who, inspired by their faith, were driven to look after a lost, wandering young American.

Once, I even tried to join them in their fast. I woke before dawn, eating a meal and drinking glass after glass of water. As the day wore on, I found myself woozy and exhausted, Istanbul's enervating heat exacerbating my hunger. I was filled with admiration for my friends, who fasted for a month straight without complaint.

If one knows anything about Turkish culture, they understand what a sacrifice fasting is. Turks love to eat, and they love to share food. In our little office, making and drinking our afternoon cup of Turkish coffee felt like a religious ceremony. But for a month, my friends gave it all up as an act of penance—a reminder of human fragility and the bounty Allah provides.

I was never more appreciative of that bounty—and my own fragility— than when, after nearly 15 hours without food or water, I tore into my first puffy, still-warm piece of Ramazan pide.

Justin Pahl is a grant writer and copy editor. He co-authored the memoir, *The Most Unlikely Champion.*

"ONE MIGHT FAST AND HE GETS NOTHING FROM HIS FAST BUT HUNGER. ONE MIGHT PRAY AT NIGHT BUT HE GETS NOTHING FROM HIS PRAYER BUT FATIGUE."

Prophet Muhammad
peace be upon him

GOAL SETTING
WITH FASTING

by Farah Dualeh

I work as a development coach which means I often work with clients to achieve their goals in a way that makes sense for them.

Goal setting – but also understanding our barriers in achieving those goals – is something many of us can struggle with.

Why do we struggle? The reason so many of us struggle with this is because we have become "too busy" to truly know what we want, why we want it, and what achieving it would give to us. We struggle with understanding our values and creating the moments of silence we need, to hear ourselves, but also the time and dedication to execute an action plan that helps us achieve those goals.

For me, Ramadan is that time of year, where I can take a break from overeating, filling my time with TV, socializing, or even all those extra hours in the office.

I use this time to reflect, pause, forgive, pray, and set my goals for the year ahead. I combine this "goal setting" with prayer which is heightened in Ramadan for those who practise it.

In the UK where I've spent most of my life, Ramadan proves to be a special time for all communities. People get involved in connecting with their neighbors, breaking iftaar with one another (all welcome) and collectively increasing charity giving.

Muslim? Non-Muslim? It doesn't matter; how will you get involved in Ramadan this year?

Farah Dualeh is the founder of Inspire Her Coaching. She is the author of *Taking Control: A Muslim Woman's Guide to Surviving Infertility.*

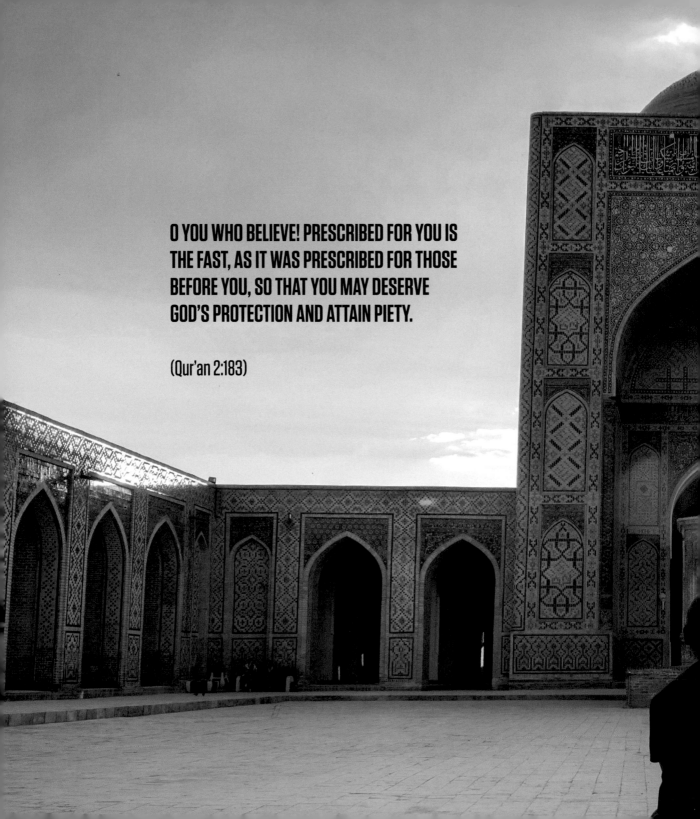

O YOU WHO BELIEVE! PRESCRIBED FOR YOU IS THE FAST, AS IT WAS PRESCRIBED FOR THOSE BEFORE YOU, SO THAT YOU MAY DESERVE GOD'S PROTECTION AND ATTAIN PIETY.

(Qur'an 2:183)

Kalyan Mosque, Bukhara, Uzbekistan

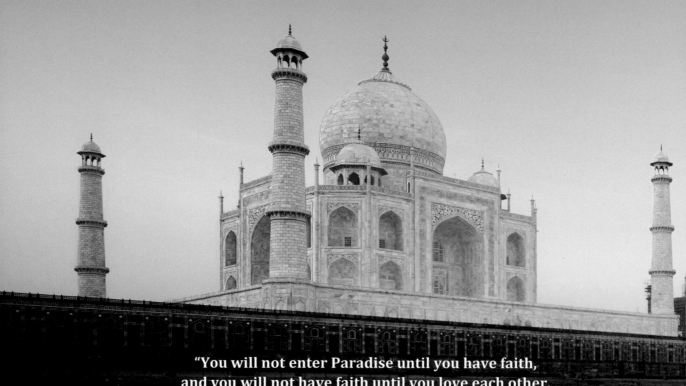

"You will not enter Paradise until you have faith,
and you will not have faith until you love each other.
Shall I show you something that, if you did, you would love each other?
Spread peace among yourselves."

Prophet Muhammad
peace be upon him

Taj Mahal Agra, India

RAMADAN
AT A GLANCE

1. Ramadan is the ninth month of the Islamic lunar calendar.

2. The Qur'anic revelation started first in Ramadan.

3. Fasting in Ramadan is one of the five pillars of Islam (others are testimony of faith, daily prayers, charity, pilgrimage)

4. Fasting starts at dawn and ends at sunset.

5 A pre-dawn meal (suhoor) is recommended and believed to be virtuous.

6. One should not put off breaking the fast (iftar).

7. Eating with family, inviting guests, and especially feeding the poor are strongly advised.
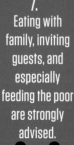

8. One must take precautions against eating too much when breaking the fast (iftar)

9. Fasting does not mean just staying hungry, but also keeping desires and actions under control.

10. Tarawih is a special prayer that is only observed during Ramadan.

11 Ramadan is not only for fasting, but also for prayer, reflection, and studying the Qur'an.

12. A three-day festival (eid al-fitr) is celebrated at the end of Ramadan.

A DAY IN RAMADAN

3 - 4 *am*

- *Wake up before dawn for suhoor – the early breakfast*
- *Wash for ablutions to stand for prayers (tahajjud), read the Qur'an, say dhikr.*
- *Take your last bits of food and drinks (better not go to extremes!)*

5 - 6 *am*

- *Morning prayer (fajr)*

7 - 8 *am*

- *Head to school, work, or, if you don't have to, take a nap!*

7 - 8 *pm*

- *Break the fast (iftar dinner) (better if start with a date or water)*
- *Evening prayer (maghrib)*
- *Tea time!*

9 - 10 *pm*

- *Tarawih prayer (better at the mosque)*

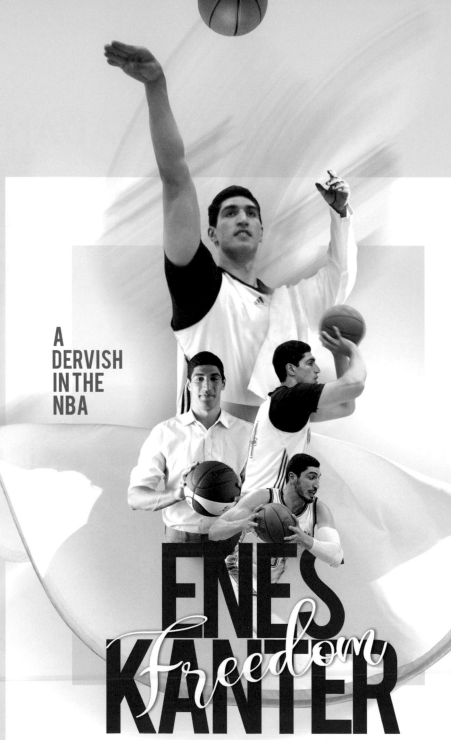

A
DERVISH
IN THE
NBA

ENES KANTER
Freedom

Healing with Fasting

FREEDOM
WITH FASTING

by Enes Kanter Freedom

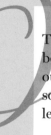

"RAMADAN IS ABOUT RELAXING YOUR BODY, YOUR SOUL, AND FOCUSING ON YOUR INNER PEACE AND EMPATHY FOR OTHERS."

Enes Kanter Freedom
NBA player, Boston Celtics
www.blazersedge.com

Our names are an important part of who we are. They indicate our parents' love for us and serve as a bond between us and our values, which help build up our identity. We love it even more if we are named after somebody or something that have made a difference and left an honorable legacy.

"What's in a name?" we sometimes ask, for what really matters is the person, regardless of labels, which names sometimes are.

I cannot agree more; but we learn from studies in psychology that our names, which were given to us when we were unable to choose on our own, have far-reaching effects in our lives than we can imagine.

I recently added "Freedom" to my last name.

I wanted Freedom to be a part of my official identity when I became an American citizen in November 2021. I wanted this change, because, well, being free is something I would not be able to enjoy if I were to step in my beloved homeland, Turkey. I wanted this change, because I dedicated an important slice of my life off the court for the last few years to voicing the struggles of freedom in Turkey and around the world.

Freedom, however, is not only about being able criticize a tyrant at home or abroad. Freedom is what makes being human inherently unique, and Ramadan is one of the best reminders for believers of this quality. True freedom is when we can overcome our selves to reveal our amazing potential each of us possess as a God-given gift.

In Ramadan, the daily routine is different than the rest of the year. Like millions of Muslims around the world, I wake up around 3 am for an early light breakfast (suhur) before the dawn arrives, after which we close our mouths for any food intake. And, to the curious question in your head, yes, we don't drink any water, too ☺

By the way, while fasting our mouths are not closed to food or water only; a Muslim should not be using any bad language, which is a foul play on the Ramadan court.

"THE LEVEL OF CLARITY DURING RAMADAN WAS JUST ALWAYS INSANE — THE WAY I CAN THINK AND TAKE IN INFORMATION."

Tareq Azim, N.F.L. trainer

www.nytimes.com/2019/05/05/sports

As I wait for the morning prayer (fajr), I read a portion from the Holy Qur'an, open my hands to the All-Merciful One, and offer my thanks for this amazing gift of life. I remember and pray for the well-being of the poor who spend days hungry as I prepare to deprive myself from food until sundown. I remember and pray for the freedom of the innocents around the world as I prepare to free myself from anger, vile thoughts, and arrogance. True incarceration is when we are locked up by our carnal desires. Those who can master over them are the freest in spirit even if their body is behind bars.

I remember Gandhi, who said during his fight for freedom:

"You can chain me, you can torture me, you can even destroy this body, but you will never imprison my mind."

I remember one of the best Turkish novelists Ahmet Altan who wrote while still in prison:

"I have never woken up in prison – not once. They may have the power to imprison me, but no one has the power to keep me in prison. Wherever you lock me up I will travel the world with the wings of my endless mind ... Like all writers, I have magic. I can pass through walls with ease."

Sports require physical strength – a lot of physical strength! – and focus. Fasting is one of the best tools to rejuvenate our bodies and to free our minds. Once free from secondary – and mostly unnecessary – thoughts, we can achieve better in everything we do. NFL trainer Tareq Azim says, "The level of clarity during Ramadan was just always insane — the way I can think and take in information."

NBA legend Hakeem Olajuwon performed some of his best when he was fasting in Ramadan. Hakeem won "player of the month" in February 1995, when he was observing Ramadan. He said, "Fasting is a spiritual mindset that gives you the stamina required to play. Through Allah's mercy, I always felt stronger and more energetic during Ramadan."

I am thankful to see such examples before me and I feel more empowered for the challenge that comes with fasting and the challenge on the court.

***

When the sun sets and I sit to break my fast – which sometimes happen as instantaneously as a "fast break" – I am filled with joy and gratitude for the priceless blessings on the table: a glass of water, a small date, and my freedom.

Enes Kanter Freedom is an NBA player and human rights activist.

> # "FASTING IS A SPIRITUAL MINDSET THAT GIVES YOU THE STAMINA REQUIRED TO PLAY. THROUGH ALLAH'S MERCY, I ALWAYS FELT STRONGER AND MORE ENERGETIC DURING RAMADAN."
>
> ## Hakeem Olajuwon
> ## NBA Hall of Famer
>
> ### www.undefeated.com

God Almighty said

"EVERY DEED OF THE CHILDREN OF ADAM IS FOR THEM, EXCEPT FOR FASTING. IT IS FOR ME AND I WILL REWARD IT."

Sahih al-Bukhari 1904,
Sahih Muslim 1151

MERCY
WITH FASTING
by M. Fethullah Gülen

For believers, Ramadan comes with incessant joy, everlasting pleasure and never fading love. The days and nights of Ramadan embrace our hearts with exclusive bliss, compassion, and love, and excite us with an enthusiasm for life.

Ramadan is the sum of our spiritual joys and the helix of the divine light for our spiritual progress. It is indeed an immense sphere of opportunity to uncover all human potentialities.

In Ramadan we are reunited with parts of society that have fallen out of touch with one another, opening the way for all those in solitude to congregate, eliminating their severance from society.

Ramadan, above all, is the month of the Qur'an; even the ones who have distanced themselves from the Qur'an throughout the year find themselves in its radiating ambience. With the spiritual joy that comes by meeting with the Qur'an again, they start sensing the entire cosmos

by and through the Qur'an, appreciating the whole of creation in reverence.

The heavenly contents of the Qur'an can be discovered only by those who can discern the sounds of the entire cosmos in its pages, but who are also attuned to the melody of the human soul; a melody composed of fear and hope, worry and joy, dolor and cheer, all at the same time. These souls who can transcend their time and listen to the Qur'an as if it has been sent just for them, can experience the flavor of paradisical fruits, the colors and beauty and the panoramic falls of the gardens and bays of Paradise, and become enthusiastic and energized.

In Ramadan one can perceive the Qur'an's celestial origin from beyond the heavens, with its divine manifestations scattered throughout the cosmos, the love of the divine emanating from it, and the traces of its glow reflecting so clearly on the countenances of the believers.

Again, within Ramadan, every single soul becomes purified from all his/her spiritual errors in an unprecedented dimension. This month grants such an abundance that everyone that shelters in its shade can benefit from its wealth and riches and attain the spiritual sultanate unlike any other. Even the most obstinate ones cannot resist and surrender to the unique ambiance of Ramadan.

An exceptional mildness and warmth embrace our conscience as we comprehend Ramadan in its original profundity... a sweet breeze of emotions blows here and there... and it, like a familiar breath, reveals numerous occasions of love and reunion!

The nights in Ramadan stand on the horizon enveloped in a mystery of silence; they whisper to us of a private meeting with the Beloved; they lead us to transcendental ways of life and present compositions of paradisical melodies for those who are capable of hearing them. The nights keep on revealing things, no matter if we can comprehend them or not. Like circles joining one

Sultanahmet and Hagia Sophia - Istanbul, Turkey

another, these mysterious utterances sometimes turn out to be such impressive orations that all hold their tongues and stand in astonishment while listening to these sermons that consist of neither letters nor words.

Even if we were to be deprived, literally, of the luminous climate of such a Ramadan, we could picture the vicinities of the mosques with their gleaming lamps that in a way recall the heavens, the faces of believers with their saint-like glow, that fill the mosques, their hearts resounding in sincerity, and their pulses beating with excitement. Their faces are shaped by trust; they throw warm-hearted glances freely on all; they shower smiles on everyone with warm hearts

open to all. These people of virtue go to the mosques with great enthusiasm to worship, and they bend their bodies double with feelings of servanthood.

Ramadan, with its light and mystery, makes all of us appreciate the spiritual riches hidden within ourselves. It feeds our starving hearts with heavenly gifts and removes all the hatred in our hearts with its blessed atmosphere.

M. Fethullah Gülen is an Islamic scholar and author of
The Messenger of God: Muhammad.

When one of you is fasting,

DO NOT SPEAK IN AN UGLY WAY

DO NOT BEHAVE IGNORANTLY

**IF INSULTED OR PROVOKED TO FIGHT
SAY "I AM FASTING."**

Prophet Muhammad
peace be upon him

I JOIN MUSLIMS DURING RAMADAN
AS A CHRISTIAN

by Craig Considine

I remember my first Ramadan experience quite well. It actually unfolded over the course of the entire month. The year was 2008. I was a 22-year-old serving as the Film Director for Ambassador Akbar Ahmed's Journey into America film project. Our academic and spiritual journey across the length and breadth of the US at the beginning of Ramadan aimed at building bridges between Muslim Americans and their fellow citizens. If I remember correctly, I attended an iftar every single day.

Since that first month-long Ramadan experience in 2008, I have been enriched by other experiences and occasions. For example, as a PhD student at Trinity College Dublin in 2012, I spent several days with Ireland-born Sufis of Pakistani ancestry. I was across the Atlantic Ocean in a completely different city, but the Ramadan vibe of hospitality and service was still there.

The Ramadan hospitality shown to me throughout the years is second-to-none. Muslim communities around the world have opened their doors to me in a genuine embrace of brotherly love and humanity. Aside from the delicious food, I particularly enjoy the company and conversations. There are few things more powerful than breaking bread together.

The service to community that I have also witnessed during Ramadan provides me with so much hope for the future of our planet. I have seen the tremendous generosity exhibited by Muslims selflessly giving their hard-earned money to various charitable causes. Regardless of the racial or religious backgrounds of human beings in need, Muslims around the world are able and willing to assist those who are suffering.

I also greatly value that act and practice of fasting, which livens my spirit and connects me more closely to my Creator. As a Christian, I fast because Jesus fasted. I join Muslims during Ramadan because embracing our humanity is what Jesus calls upon me to do.

Dr. Craig Considine is an award-winning professor and the best-selling author of *The Humanity of Muhammad - A Christian View.*

FASTING ON
RAMADAN
& YOM KIPPUR

By Rabbi Allen S. Maller

Ka'ba, Mecca, Saudi Arabia

I am a Reform rabbi who has been studying Islam for more than 50 years. Reform Judaism is the largest branch of the three major denominations of Jews in America. I think it is vitally important for our generation to understand how much Islam and Judaism have in common, and fasting is one area where this harmony is evident. In the U.S. and Canada, Jews and Muslims are the religious groups that noticeably practice fasting. There are several religious values involved in fasting; Muslims will see many similarities, and a few differences, in the following teachings from the Jewish tradition.

Don't most people think that being happy is the most important thing? Isn't eating one of the most accessible pleasures we have? Why should people limit their culinary pleasures? More outrageous, why should we afflict ourselves by fasting? Why do Islam and Judaism restrict their adherents from the simple pleasure of food each year? For the entire month of Ramadan, Muslims fast from first light until sundown, abstaining from food, drink and marital relations. The Qur'an says, "Oh you who believe! Fasting is prescribed to you as it was prescribed to those before you, that you may (learn) self-restraint" (2:183). Why should the Torah decree for Jews a day of fasting (Leviticus 16:29, 23:27) when for twenty-four hours adult Jews (in good health) are supposed to trouble their bodies by abstaining from eating, drinking and marital relations? Both religions teach us that what we do not eat may be even more important than what we do eat.

All animals eat, but only humans choose not to eat some foods that are both nutritious and tasty. Some people do not eat meat for religious or ethical reasons. Jews and Muslims do not eat pork for religious and spiritual reasons. On fast days such as Yom Kippur—the Day of Atonement and the ninth of Av (a day of mourning like the Shi'a observance of Ashura on the tenth of Muharram)—Jews do not eat or drink anything at all, and abstain from marital relations for twenty-four hours. Fasting results in many different outcomes that help bring us closer to God.

First of all, fasting teaches compassion. It is easy to talk about the world's problem of hunger, easy to feel sorry that millions of people go to bed hungry each day. But not until one actually feels it in one's own body does the impact truly hit home. Compassion based on empathy is much stronger and more consistent than compassion based on pity. It is a feeling that leads to action. Fasting is never an end in itself; it has many different outcomes. But none of the other outcomes are of real moral value if compassion is not enlarged and extended through fasting. As the prophet Isaiah said, "The truth is that at the same time you fast, you pursue your own interests and oppress your workers. Your fasting makes you violent, and you quarrel and fight. The kind of fasting I want is this: remove the chains of oppression and the yoke of injustice, and let the oppressed go free. Share your food with the hungry and open your homes to the homeless poor" (Isaiah 58:3-7).

Second, fasting is an exercise in will power. Many people think they can't fast because it's too difficult, but actually the discomfort of hunger pangs is relatively minor. A headache, muscle soreness from too much exercise, or a toothache are more severe than the pain temporary hunger produces. I have on one occasion fasted for three days, and found that after the first twenty-four hours the pain decreases slightly, as the stomach becomes numb. The real reason it is challenging to fast is because it so easy to break the fast, since food is almost always in easy reach — all you have to do is take a bite. Thus the key to fasting is the will power to decide again and again not to eat or drink. Our society has increasingly become one of self-indulgence; we lack basic self-discipline. Fasting opposes our increasing "softness" in life; when people exercise their will power to fast, they are affirming their self-control and celebrating mastery over themselves. We

need continually to prove to ourselves that we can do it, because we are aware of our frequent failures to be self-disciplined.

The third outcome of fasting is improved physical health. Of course, one twenty-four hour fast will not have any more effect than one day of exercise; only prolonged and regular fasting promotes health. The annual fast on Yom Kippur can, however, awaken us to the importance of how much and how often we eat. For many years, research has shown that when animals are slightly underfed, receiving a balanced diet below the normal quantity for maximum physical health, their life spans were prolonged from 50 to 100 percent. With all the additives placed in food these days, a reduction of total food intake is healthful. More important, since our society has problems with overabundance, fasting provides a good lesson in the virtue of denial. Illnesses caused by overeating are increasing in affluent Western countries, such as the incidence of diabetes. Sixteen million people in the United States have diabetes, according to the U.S. Centers for Disease Control and Prevention.

Diabetes can lead to blindness, kidney disease, heart disease, nerve damage, amputation and sometimes death. The prevalence of the disease is related to high rates of obesity and sedentary lifestyles, which increase the risk of developing the disease. More than half of adults in Los Angeles are overweight, and 60 percent do not get regular exercise. One-fifth of all those who are obese will develop diabetes. Thus going without any food, or even water, for a twenty-four hour period challenges us to think about the benefits of the spiritual doctrine "less is more."

Fourth in our list of outcomes is that fasting is a positive struggle against our dependencies. We live in a consumer society, and are constantly bombarded by advertising that tells us we must

have this or that to be healthy, happy, popular, or wise. By fasting, we assert that we need not be totally reliant on external, material things, even essentials such as food. If our most basic need for food and drink can be suspended for twenty-four hours, how much more may we learn to limit our needs for all non-essentials? Judaism and Islam do not advocate asceticism as an end in itself; in fact, it's against Jewish and Muslim law to deny ourselves normal physical pleasures. But in our overheated consumer society, it is necessary periodically to turn off the constant pressure to consume, and forcibly remind ourselves that "Man does not live by bread alone" (Deuteronomy 8:3).

Fifth, fasting serves as a penance. Though self-inflicted pain may alleviate some guilt, it is much better to reduce one's guilt with offsetting acts of righteousness. This is why charity is an important part of Yom Kippur, and the same is true for Muslims during Ramadan. Indeed, Judaism teaches that fasting which doesn't increase compassion is ignored by God. The concept of fasting as penance helps us to understand that our hunger pains can be beneficial. Contemporary culture desires happiness and comfort above all else. Any pain or suffering is

FASTING IS GOOD FOR THE SOUL. IT OFTEN SERVES AS AN AID FOR SPIRITUAL EXPERIENCES. FOR MOST PEOPLE, ESPECIALLY THOSE WHO HAVE NOT FASTED REGULARLY BEFORE, HUNGER PAINS ARE A DISTRACTION.

seen as unnecessary, even evil. Though we occasionally hear people echo values from the past that suffering can help one grow, or that an existence unalloyed with grief would lack certain qualities of greatness, many today think that the primary goal in life is to always be happy and free from all discomfort. The satisfaction one derives from the self-induced pain of fasting provides insight into a better possible reaction to the normal, external suffering we will all experience throughout our lives. Taking a pill is not always the best way to alleviate pain, especially if by doing so we allay the symptoms without reaching the root cause.

Sixth, fasting is good for the soul. It often serves as an aid for spiritual experiences. For most people, especially those who have not fasted regularly before, hunger pains are a distraction. People who are not by nature spiritual or emotional individuals will probably find that a one-day fast is insufficient to induce an altered state of consciousness. Those who have fasted regularly on Yom Kippur might like to try a two- to three-day fast (liquids permitted after the first 24 hours). It is best to go about daily activities and devote late evening or early morning to meditation and prayer. Having already fasted for Yom Kippur, one may simply extend the fast another thirty-six to forty-eight hours. We are prohibited to fast prior to Yom Kippur; eating a good meal prior to Yom Kippur Eve is a mitzvah (religious duty), because Judaism, like Islam, opposes excessive asceticism.

The seventh outcome of fasting is the performance of a mitzvah, which is the one fundamental reason for fasting on Yom Kippur. We do carry out mitzvot (religious duties) in order to benefit ourselves, but because our duty as Jews requires us to do them. Fasting is a very personal mitzvah, with primarily personal consequences. Fasting on Yom Kippur is a personal offering to God, from each and every Jew who fasts. For more than 100 generations, Jews have fasted on this day; fasting is part of the Jewish people's covenant with God. The principal reason to fast is to fulfill God's commandment, but the outcome of the fast can be any of a half-dozen forms of self-fulfillment. But simply knowing that one has done one's duty as a faithful Jew is the most basic and primary outcome of all.

Finally, fasting should be combined with the study of Torah (the five books of Moses specifically, or Scriptural texts in general). A medieval text states, "Better to eat a little and study twice as much, for the study of Torah is superior to fasting." Indeed, the more one studies, the less one needs to fast. Fasting is a very personal, experiential offering. However, though study is also a personal experience, it takes place with a text and/or a teacher. The Divine will is often more readily and truly experienced in study or in spiritual dialogue with others than in solitary meditation.

May our fasting become a first step toward the removal of the chains of self-oppression and narrow-mindedness that enslave us, our neighbors, and our world! May future years of shared fasting by Muslims and Jews lead to a greater understanding and respect through increased acceptance of religious pluralism. May we always be part of those organizations and movements that are fully committed to contributing to world peace, and who are equally committed to respecting both our own religion and our neighbor's.

Muslim scholar Fethullah Gülen points out that the Abrahamic faiths (Judaism, Christianity, and Islam) and some non-Abrahamic faiths (Hinduism) accept that there is only One source for all religions, and pursue the same goal. Gülen states: "As a Muslim, I accept all Prophets and Books sent to different peoples throughout history, and regard belief in them as an essential principle of being Muslim. A Muslim is a true follower of Abraham, Moses, David, Jesus, and all other Prophets. Not believing in one Prophet or Book means that one is not a Muslim. Thus we acknowledge the oneness and basic unity of religion, which is a symphony of God's blessings and mercy, and the universality of belief in religion." Gülen's description of universal religion as a symphony is an excellent illustration. One cannot have harmony if everyone plays the same notes; and one cannot have symphony if everyone plays the same instruments. Individual conductors and composers are different, but the source of musical creativity is One. According to a hadith narrated by Abu Huraira, Prophet Muhammad said, "The prophets are paternal brothers; their mothers are different, yet their religion is one (because they all have the same father)" (Bukhari, Book 55, Hadith 652).

Rabbi Allen S. Maller is has published over 100 articles on Jewish values in popular magazines; Jewish, Muslim and Christian. He is the author of *Tikunay Nefashot*.

THE PERFECT MISSION FOR A SUPERHERO

by Sana Khan

The night before the big day was finally here. It felt like the longest countdown in the history of countdowns—because it was. Eleven months of looking forward to something was probably the hardest thing I had ever done. You see, all these years my life had been rainbows and unicorns. But now that I was officially double-digits, it was time to take on larger missions. Like my friend Ahmed says, what kind of superheroes save only half the world? He is so right and that's why we decided to fast all thirty days of Ramadan instead of the fifteen we were allowed last year. Our parents kept telling us to take it one fast at a time, but I think everyone knew we had already made up our minds. With us, nothing was ever halfway. We either didn't do something, or went all the way. This was going to be the most epic Ramadan of our lives!

"Hey. Ready?" I watched the floating bubbles on the screen. Ahmed was still working on his typing skills.

"So ready. Mom just gave me my note. You have

yours?" We realized two weeks ago that the first day of Ramadan was also the day of our class field trip. Mrs. Wilson requested a note from our parents so she wouldn't order hot lunches for us. When she had first heard we wouldn't be eating or drinking anything all day, her eyebrows shot up so high they almost disappeared under her hair. It made our mission feel even more worth it.

"Yep. See you tomorrow!" It was 9—the hour we had decided to be in bed if we stood a chance at this. As Ahmed says, preparation is half of success. He should totally write a book one day. But probably get someone else to do the typing for him.

"Faez. FAEZ." Mama tried to whisper but it was so loud I almost jumped out of bed. My little brother moved under the blanket and Mama put her hand over my shoulder, freezing in position. "C'mon, we only have an hour before Suhoor ends."

I put on my superhero cape and flew out of bed. I had already put toothpaste on my toothbrush the night before. Every Suhoor

minute was worth its weight in gold. You can probably guess who said that.

My plate was ready and waiting on the table. Mama was pretty good at this superhero thing. For my very first Suhoor of the most epic Ramadan, I had asked for my favorites—kebab with rice, chocolate croissant, and a vanilla ice-cream milkshake. Mama warned me it may all be too much, but I told her I could handle it. Double-digits meant a bigger appetite, right?

Wrong. A few bites later my stomach felt like I had swallowed the table. Mama looked at me with a told-you-so expression on her face, but said nothing. Instead, she smiled and gave me a big glass of water. "Drink up. 15 minutes to go."

The fast hadn't even started but it already felt hard. Remember, the beginning is always the toughest. The glass of water stared at me, daring me to quit. I pulled my cape tighter and sat up straight. The superhero juice flowed right to my muscles and I could feel my powers coming back. Let's do this.

6:05 AM. 12 hours and 17 minutes to go.

Fajr Salah had given me more superpowers because I felt like I could run a marathon. But Mama told me to go back to sleep right away. She said this extra hour before school would make a big difference at the end of the day. And she had been kind of right about Suhoor. I was learning superheroes-in-training aren't above taking advice. Note to self: must include this in Ahmed's all-time bestseller.

7:15 AM. 11 hours and 7 minutes.

Okay, so I am not going to tell you I felt awesome as I ran to catch my bus. My cape felt like a popped balloon. I was tired and my mouth felt dry. This wasn't all too bad, but just then something strange happened. I started to hear my heartbeat in my ears, as loud as the marching band drums, and my palms became all sweaty. I was panicking and my superhero self was nowhere to be found. 11 hours flashed in bright red lights on a huge scoreboard.

"Hey! How was Suhoor?" I could literally see Ahmed standing tall with his arms across his chest, his cape flowing perfectly behind him.

"Hey." I sat down next to him, hoping some of his powers would rub off on me. "Good, and you?"

"So great. Can't wait. To break my fast with the yummy date." He burst out laughing. Normally I would laugh at his silly poetry. But now I laughed with him, hoping it would take my mind off the flashing scoreboard.

9 AM. 9 hours and 22 minutes.

"Woah, you mean you guys can't even drink water all day?" Chris asked and the whole class turned to look at me and Ahmed. Two bright spotlights beamed down on us, almost making me forget about the scoreboard and the fire-breathing dragon in my chest.

"Nope, no water, no food," I said, swallowing hard. The spitting cobra had better not make me burp right now. Second note to self: NO MORE spicy kebabs for Suhoor!

Mrs. Wilson took our notes and told us we could let her know when we needed to pray or rest throughout the day. She even offered to let us go back in the air-conditioned bus if we needed. Hey, maybe this day would turn out to be alright after all.

11:30 AM. 6 hours and 52 minutes.

Pizza!? What happened to the rice and beans they made us eat on days we were taking state tests? The fire in my chest was long gone, only to be replaced by something that was much worse—HUNGER. TO THE NEXT LEVEL.

I wished Mrs. Wilson had sent us to the bus before the pizza arrived. But not more than I wished to take just one bite of that hot...gooey...melty cheese—

"Hey, you wanna go hang out in the bus? The tires are flat and there are crying kindergartners who could really use our help." Ahmed put on his best smile. I remembered he was lactose intolerant. Just being in the same room as cheese made his stomach hurt.

"Can I come with you guys?" Chris called out. "I am not that hungry anyway."

I had known Chris since we were five and I knew he loved pizza too. He walked to the bus with us and I saw him take quick bites out of a napkin he was hiding behind his back. I pretended not to look, but what Chris did was so cape-worthy.

2:12 PM. 4 hours and 10 minutes.

"How are you doing, Faez?" Mama had already started cooking Iftar.

I wanted to tell her I was STARVING and could eat all her chicken—and the pot. But of course, that's not what I actually said.

"I am okay, Mama." Wait, doesn't lying in Ramadan break your fast?

Super-Heroing on an empty stomach was seriously giving me pudding brain, but technically, I was okay. Until—

Did someone say pudding? Mama's creamy rice pudding with rosewater would be real ni—

Mayday, Mayday! I raced to find the Champion's Manual we had written for this very emergency. It was time to get my superpowers back.

Qur'an recitation was Number One on the list. Something about reciting out loud, pretending we were famous reciters made us feel pretty great. And it worked. I even spent some time playing with my little brother afterwards. And it wasn't just because I knew the reward for a charity done in this month was seventy times more than any other day of the year. Although I have to admit, that was a pretty big bonus.

5:30 PM. 52 minutes.

The Homestretch—also known as M.A.M.A (Max Alert for Mission Abort). If I stood the slightest chance at the finish line, I had to get my nose and my eyes FAR away from the kitchen. And my ears too because I was sure I heard the chicken shawarmas calling my name! Before any other body parts betrayed me, I dashed out to join the rest of my squad.

6:22 PM. MISSION ACCOMPLISHED.

The cool water in my mouth felt like heaven and the date tasted sweeter than candy.

Then suddenly, it occurred to me.

As awesome as the finish line felt, the battles I had been fighting all day were the real stuff of superheroes. With a little (okay, a lot of) help—hey, who said superheroes had to do it all alone—I had defeated Hunger, Thirst, Impatience, Anger and Fear.

Could there be a better mission for a real superhero?

Sana Khan is a writer of stories inspired from the Qur'an. She is a physician in Texas and holds a degree in English literature.

A LIFE
WITH FASTING

by Hakan Yesilova

To the pleasure-obsessed mind, fasting does not make much sense. How come and why would anybody forsake his or her morning coffee, lunch break, or tea with cookies on the side (unless our doctors tell us to do)?

This is exactly what Muslims do every year for an entire month – not for health reasons, but for faith reasons.

Fasting in the month of Ramadan is one of the essential duties in Islam. This duty is not just about remaining hungry whole day, just as worship in any form is not (or should not be) merely physical exercise. Fasting serves best when we can "fast from our material world" to reinforce our spiritual world. Our religious traditions – at least that's the case in Islam – are teaching us to seek a balance between our physical and spiritual needs; both need to be satisfied, both need to have their weight on the scale. But many of us live our lives like a rat race to bring home bread, to pursue career ambitions that fill our whole time, and many of us do not even have a minute to have some serious deep contemplation about who we are, why we are here in this life, and what our purpose is. The holy month of Ramadan offers such an opportunity for those who can manage to withdraw a bit from their hectic life.

Muslims hope at the end of Ramadan to have been reformed, bodily, spiritually, and in character, that they have become better than what they were before. Prophet Muhammad, peace be upon him, said "One might fast and he gets nothing from his fast but hunger. One might pray at night but he gets nothing from his prayer but fatigue." Without truly transforming in behavior, fasting, and all acts of worship for that matter, become only ritual, family tradition, diet, or physical exercise. Such a transformation is what falls on the side of believers, for God does what we expect from His infinite Mercy by clearing up the path for us: The Prophet says, "When Ramadan comes, devils are chained up, the gates of fire are closed, and the gates of paradise are open." We fail this opportunity if we are tempted to go near the fire instead of paradise.

Fasting is a state of being year-round. Believers are always expected to fast from bad behavior, over-consumption, greed, hatred, bad words, injustice, and eating certain things. We fast from our weaknesses and our trespassing desires. The holy month of Ramadan is a reminder that by observing our limits we can establish harmony and ensure social order. The Prophet advises believers to stay away from conflict; when they are provoked to fight or argue during Ramadan, he teaches them just to say, "I am fasting." He also encourages to be generous and helping others in need. In the month of Ramadan, the Prophet "was more nourishing than the fast wind." By "fasting" from our passions throughout the year and not allowing biological composition to dominate over us, we can attain true inner and outer peace.

Reconnecting with the cosmos

To the modern human, whose life is fixated with linear working hours and

MANY OF US LIVE OUR LIVES LIKE A RAT RACE TO BRING HOME BREAD, TO PURSUE CAREER AMBITIONS THAT FILL OUR WHOLE TIME, AND MANY OF US DO NOT EVEN HAVE A MINUTE TO HAVE SOME SERIOUS DEEP CONTEMPLATION ABOUT WHO WE ARE, WHY WE ARE HERE IN THIS LIFE, AND WHAT OUR PURPOSE IS. THE HOLY MONTH OF RAMADAN OFFERS SUCH AN OPPORTUNITY FOR THOSE WHO CAN MANAGE TO WITHDRAW A BIT FROM THEIR HECTIC LIFE.

classes, Ramadan is somewhat a major disruption. Muslims determine the beginning of Ramadan with the sight of the new moon and observe it until the next crescent. They wake up and have their early breakfast before the dawn; they break their fast with the sunset. Sense of time becomes realigned with the cosmic time of celestial beings. In this sense, Ramadan helps us reconnect with the universe, for in Islamic tradition the human being is like the microcosm, the index or matrix of the universe, whereas the universe is like a macro-human. What looks like a disruption to the modern human is in fact a reminder of our being part of the cosmic reality. Maybe such a "disruption" is something we need, for life is more than repeated stillness and we need change as much as we need continuity.

Ramadan during the pandemic

As sad and tragic as it was, the pandemic era has influenced our approach to worship, too. Thankfully, we are now able to congregate in our places of worship, but for two years many of us observed our otherwise collective prayers at home. As we pray for the loss of many who died due to Covid-19, we also need to think what the divine wisdom might have been behind this what appears to be the

Healing with Fasting

smallest killer of all time, which is not even a living thing. What might be the wisdom that we were all grounded in our homes, and our mosques, churches, and temples were not open for services?

I spoke with many friends about their Ramadan experience at home. An overwhelming majority said it was one of the best they ever had. Of course, we missed hugging friends, enjoying iftar meals together, and praying the tarawih at the mosque. But during lockdown in homes, we discovered something we probably were missing at other times: the true depth of prayer at an individual level. This depth manifests itself when we can focus – and solitude is sometimes the best tool to reinstall our factory settings, to remember our true human nature. This is why many mystics seek to retreat from society to be able to listen to the inner call that is innately there and we humans under the conditions of our modern lifestyles are too busy to hear that divine voice. Turning our home into a place of worship – not only to school or office – in times of quarantine is one of the best things we can do for a deeper spiritual journeying. "Quarantine," which etymologically means "forty days," reminds us of the Islamic tradition of chila or arbaeen (both meaning forty) observed by mystics to attain spiritual fulfilment. Believers turned their homes into places of worship many times in the past when they were unable to get together in their temples. According to the Qur'an, this was the case at the time Moses (pbuh) and he was told to teach his community of believers to "make their homes places to turn to God and establish prayer" (10:87) when they were being persecuted by the Pharaoh.

Fasting and diversity

Fasting is not unique to Muslims. The Qur'anic verse related to fasting in Ramadan reminds us that we are connected with other faith traditions more closely than we know: O you who believe! Prescribed for you is the Fast, as it was prescribed for those before you, so that you may deserve God's protection and attain piety (2:183).

Shield

"Fasting is a shield ..." says the Prophet, for it protects us from the "fire" by taming ourselves not to jump from self-indulgence to another. Just as we learned during the pandemic that we could actually survive with much less – be it food, toilet paper, etc. – fasting reminds us we could do quite well without gratifying our every craving. Such a "shield" is necessary for a healthy life, for our body, and for the nature, for most of what we are consuming every day are things we can do without. Fasting is also important in terms of our health, too. Fasting is a scientifically proven tool to help us just do that by revitalizing our entire body at a cellular level. Prophet Muhammad, peace be upon him, referred to this truth 1,400 years ago when he said "Fast, and you will find health."

Hakan Yesilova is the editor of *The Fountain*, a bimonthly magazine on life, knowledge, and belief

Umayyad Mosque, Damascus, Syria

Read!

**Read in the name of your lord who has created;
created the human from a clot clinging.
Read, and your lord is the all-munificent, who has
taught by the pen
Taught human what he did not know.
(Qur'an 96:1-5)**

CONFESSIONS
OF A FASTING MOM

by Hannah Matus

21 Days Before Ramadan

I happen to click on a Omar Suleiman lecture reminding his listeners to begin to prepare themselves early for Ramadan, and I make it almost ten, whole, blissfully quiet minutes in before Fatima, my two-year-old daughter, wakes up from her nap, wailing for milk. I hasten to the fridge, repeating the good advice that I managed to absorb in my mind, spilling some milk onto the counter as I do so. I absently grab the towel that hangs off of the oven handle for just such emergencies and sop it up, looking plaintively at the coffee machine as I do so. But then my daughter emits a particularly ear-splitting cry and I know there is no time for coffee. I trudge up the stairs, sippy cup in hand as I try to commit the advice to memory. Purify your heart. Fast some days the month before. Write a "Ramadan goals" list. Work on concentration in—the screeching intensifies and I finish climbing the last two stairs in a jump Olympians would envy, promising myself to revisit the lecture again soon. I still have loads of time before Ramadan….

Day 1

Beep, beep, beep, honks the relentless and constant, ever-annoying alarm ring, and it hits me in a rush. Suhoor. The first day of Ramadan, and I thank Allah in a silent alhamdullillah that I managed to actually pull myself up out of bed for it. Ramadan and coffee addictions mean suhoor, the sunnah dawn breakfast meal and technically a non-obligatory practice for Muslims, is a must. I drink my coffee in large gulps, despite a lack of appetite for it so early in the morning. I drink more after I finish eating a few dates, like it is a glass of thirst-quenching milk. I chug a bottle of water with one eye on the seconds portion of the digital clock on my smartphone. 59 seconds until fajr, the predawn prayer. My stomach shouts "no!" but I know I must to stave of dehydration for the day. I take one last gulp of water, before fajr prayer finally dawns.

Oh, and my husband is here with me, too, sitting across from me, weary, not talking much, his hair endearingly mussed from sleep, and I just know counting the seconds until he can be sleeping once again. We do not talk—

we just sit in a comfortable silence. Too tired, and quite frankly, neither of us wants to risk waking our daughter this early with our murmured conversation.

***

In the morning, after suhoor and before Fatima wakes up, the house is quiet and serene. I feel the pulse of Ramadan beating through the house. The air itself thrives with a sort of energy that doesn't seem to exist at any other time of the year. I play Quran from my phone on low volume in the background and just sit, reflecting on my goals, what acts of charity I can commit to for the month, whether I will invite guests over to break their fasts with us this year. That sense of peace buoys and envelops me throughout the day until—

Fatima throws her oatmeal with fresh blueberries I made her for breakfast in my face. Literally. I stick out my tongue to clean the blob of oatmeal off of my lip, before I remember I am fasting. Good thing, too, for I am able to stop the shout that almost escapes from my mouth. Deep breath. Calm.

"No, habibti, not nice," I say instead. I long for naptime. And then iftar. I contemplate what to cook for the first iftar this Ramadan. Soup and a slew of finger foods sound just the thing.

I race through most of my Ramadan goals for the day like a champ. I do some light exercise, read a few pages of the Quran, do a little Ramadan coloring activity with Fatima. Before iftar, I finish my Quran pages for the day. Fatima, however, can tell I am only halfway paying attention to her and takes off her diaper in protest. Unfortunately, it was not a clean one. I rush her to the bath.

Iftar starts before Fatima wakes up from her afternoon nap. My husband and I catch up in the moments before sunset on each other's days. We pray maghrib together and then sit down to eat. We manage a few bites each before Fatima wails awake. We lock eyes and almost laugh out loud. Kids have impeccable timing.

He reaches out a hand to stop me from getting up, and I finish eating alone as he leaves the table to collect our little girl.

Day 3

I don't wake up in time for suhoor today. I must survive the day without my daily dose of caffeine. I go through the motions of the day in a zombie-like state, and my daughter's terrible-two tantrum of the day grates extra roughly. I stare blankly at her for a few seconds before scooping her up and looking around for a distraction. It is a wonder how much energy these little human beings have.

I cook a light soup early in the day, and get as much done as I can even as I feel my energy slowly seeping away as the day drags on. A headache hints at its existence and becomes more and more persistent the closer it gets to iftar time.

I almost cry in relief when Fatima drifts into a nap two hours before iftar. A blessed reprieve as I allow my own head to hit the pillow. I sleep until it is time to break fast.

Day 11

I get through the first ten days making good progress with my Quran reading and praying goals. Today, though, I feel quite tired and almost forego my 8 rakat. Fatimah woke up several times the night before—teething molars.

But I would be disappointed in myself if I missed them. I pray them, but I read mostly short surahs.

Fatimah fakes me out during bedtime and climbs out of her bed mid-rakah to climb on my back. Then she grabs her pink "cloud" blanket and wraps it around her head, prostrates with her forehead to the ground mimicking me, albeit about 45 degrees off from Mecca. She makes whisper sounds as she sits back up on her knees. I try to remember what surah I had been reading.

When I end my prayer, I try not to laugh as I kiss the top of her head and place her back in bed.

Day 15

We sit at our usual place at the kitchen table during suhoor, sipping our coffee and nibbling some dates, when we hear her shout from the top of the stairs.

"Mama? Baba?" My husband and I share a resigned but amused glance as we listen to little footfalls make their way carefully down the steps, down the hall to where we sit at the kitchen table.

"Eat?" she asks, reaching for some dates. My husband pours her a glass of milk. She sits in a regular-size chair,

her legs swinging above the ground as she bites into a date, looking up at us solemnly, wondering at this curious break from her daily routine.

It is going to be a long day.

Day 20

Today, I venture out with my husband and Fatima to pray taraweeh at the masjid.

I think of how she ran gleefully around the spacious prayer area in the

women's section, one of only a handful of other children, giggling as she attempts to pilfer purses and keys strewn across the rows of praying ladies. And the sympathetic smiles of the older mothers that seem to say, been there! I am pretty sure I won't try that again this Ramadan.

Day 27

I am still so weary when I wake up at 4 in the morning. But I do not want to miss an odd night. I have done a good job of pulling myself up for prayer in the last third of the night these past few days, trying to catch the Night of Power by doing extra acts of worship. Don't give in to your tiredness now, I tell myself. I nudge my sleepy husband awake, coaxing him to wake up to pray.

I peak out the window almost unconsciously, peering out into the night sky, as if it will give me some clue.

Is this Laylat ul Qadr, the Night of Power? I wonder. The stars shimmer through a thin haze of misty clouds that drift and sway in the calm early morning breeze. I open the window a sliver to let in the cool, fresh morning air. If it is the night worth a thousand months, I want to feel like I was part of that night. I pray. I ask Allah to protect our small family. To guide and protect our daughter always. Prayers for her make up most of my duaa.

I fall asleep right away when I curl under the covers. I wake up at the usual time, a few minutes before Fatima. I expect a crashing wave of exhaustion. I get out of bed slowly, and instead feel as if I'd slept away my exhaustion for the month. I plan a busy day of buying Eid gifts for loved ones and baking sweets with Fatima, smiling in amazement at my unusual burst of energy.

My own personal miracle.

Eid Day

My husband and I trudge tiredly up the stairs after fajr prayer. Fatima calls out to us, having heard the noise, excited and energetic.

"Mama! Baba!" she calls. She hurries toward us, pulling our hands back toward the stairs, pointing at the decorations I hung at night before bed. My husband and I smile at each other and allow ourselves to be guided back down. We watch as she excitedly rips open her presents, her moon and star pajamas twinkling at us, reflecting the living room's decorative lights. Her exuberance warms my heart.

Alhamdulillah, I think, thanking Allah. Alhamdulillah a thousand times for the blessing of Ramadan spent with my little cherished family.

Hannah Matus, Esq, is a licensed attorney in Ohio. She is the author of *A Second Look*, her debut novel.

MY FIRST
TEXAS RAMADAN

by Brandon Richey

Picture it: it's May 2019, and you're working outside in the Texas heat. Playground equipment adorns the ground at your feet as you struggle to assemble a jungle gym for the kids at work. Power tools, slats of wood, and huge pieces of plastic lie scattered, baking in near-90 degree heat. Your co-worker is guzzling water from a one gallon jug, trying to make up for all the sweat he's losing to the Texas summer.

And there you are – fasting.

I had just accepted Islam in November 2018, and now six months later came the first attempt to fast all throughout the month of Ramadan. I had never associated holy months with any particular hardship or test of willpower – quite the opposite. Growing up Baptist Christian in the South, you only think of presents and candy when you think of "holy months" – Easter and Christmas being times to celebrate, rather than times to reflect. If you had tried to tell me a year ago that I would not only enjoy the experience of fasting and praying throughout a 30-day period, but that I would miss it when it was over, I would have wondered what you were currently dizzy on.

Yet, when June came and Ramadan ended, it almost felt like I was saying goodbye to something special.

There is a sort of shared experience with your fellow Muslims during Ramadan. You all understand the feelings of sleepiness, thirst, and loss of energy that comes with not eating and drinking during the day. You nod at each other as the clock passes Asr and you are thinking about that first, sweet sip of water. Time is something you are persistently aware of as you inch closer and closer to sunset.

At the same time you are overcome with a feeling of mindfulness and thanks throughout the day. It's hard to describe to someone who's never experienced Ramadan what it feels like to be so aware of not only your own body, but your own thoughts. You appreciate what you have, the friends you've made, the family you were blessed with, and know that at the end of it all we have Allah to thank for it.

I found myself spending more and more time at the mosque, not just because it felt like something to do, but because you want to be there. One night I remember waking up at 3:00 AM, and rather than sit around and munch while I had the chance I just drove to the mosque and prayed in the musalla for hours. I practiced my recitation, because by now I had finally memorized my first new surah, and the time flew by. Before I knew it the others had joined me for Fajr prayer, and we started our fast together.

It's true what you're told, though – eventually the fast becomes easy, and

you are almost thoughtlessly gliding through the day with nary a drop of water to tempt you. The consciousness of Allah, however – the taqwah – remains throughout the month. It makes even the most lackadaisical Muslim not miss prayer, and brings those who chose to worship alone into the welcoming arms of their neighbors and community.

Something else jumps out at me, too. For the longest time I've had a hard time explaining to non-Muslims the relationship between morality and faith. I don't believe faith is necessary to reach moral or ethical conclusions, however I notice that an awareness of Allah or a set of standards set by Him means that you check your behavior and thoughts more often. Am I good because the Qur'an tells me to be? Maybe not, but would I always make the most moral choices if I wasn't reminded to remember Allah in all that I do? Probably not.

Ramadan is that, but in overdrive. You are constantly wondering how you can maximize the good deeds you perform in your life, and go out of your way to help the people around you. You think of distant relatives more, friends, neighbors, people at the masjid, the sick, the needy, and the homeless. Being aware of your own discomfort drives you to

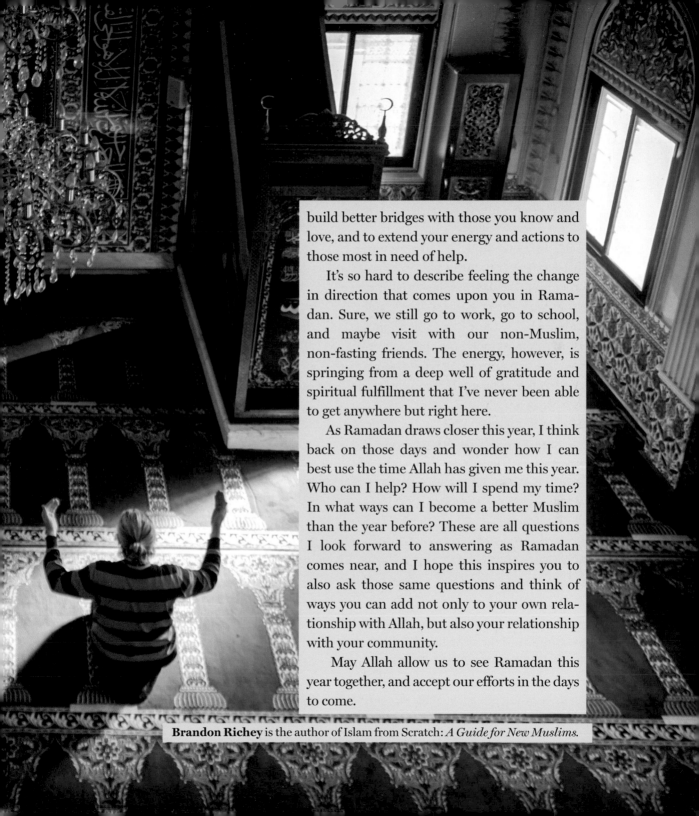

build better bridges with those you know and love, and to extend your energy and actions to those most in need of help.

It's so hard to describe feeling the change in direction that comes upon you in Ramadan. Sure, we still go to work, go to school, and maybe visit with our non-Muslim, non-fasting friends. The energy, however, is springing from a deep well of gratitude and spiritual fulfillment that I've never been able to get anywhere but right here.

As Ramadan draws closer this year, I think back on those days and wonder how I can best use the time Allah has given me this year. Who can I help? How will I spend my time? In what ways can I become a better Muslim than the year before? These are all questions I look forward to answering as Ramadan comes near, and I hope this inspires you to also ask those same questions and think of ways you can add not only to your own relationship with Allah, but also your relationship with your community.

May Allah allow us to see Ramadan this year together, and accept our efforts in the days to come.

Brandon Richey is the author of Islam from Scratch: *A Guide for New Muslims.*

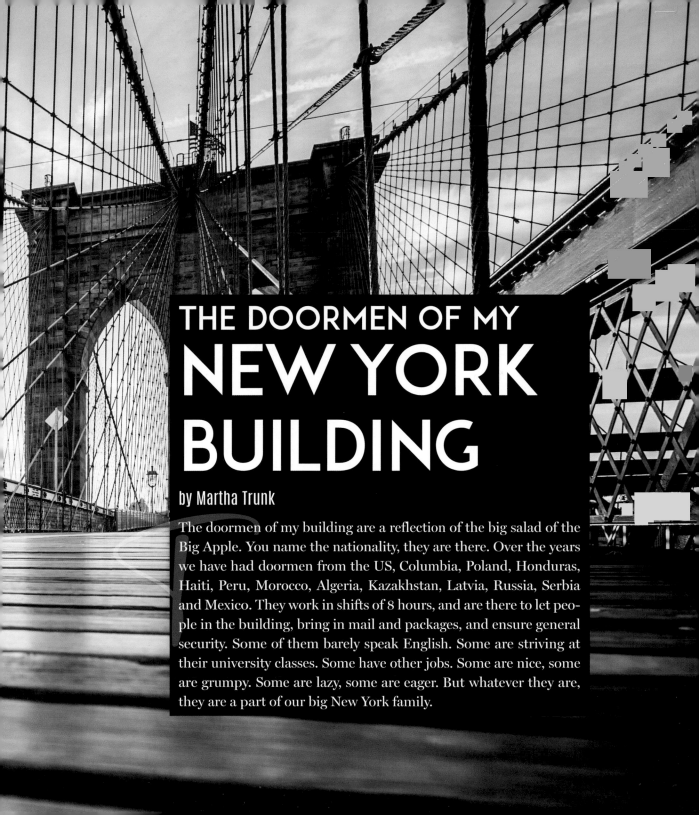

THE DOORMEN OF MY
NEW YORK
BUILDING

by Martha Trunk

The doormen of my building are a reflection of the big salad of the Big Apple. You name the nationality, they are there. Over the years we have had doormen from the US, Columbia, Poland, Honduras, Haiti, Peru, Morocco, Algeria, Kazakhstan, Latvia, Russia, Serbia and Mexico. They work in shifts of 8 hours, and are there to let people in the building, bring in mail and packages, and ensure general security. Some of them barely speak English. Some are striving at their university classes. Some have other jobs. Some are nice, some are grumpy. Some are lazy, some are eager. But whatever they are, they are a part of our big New York family.

I became friendly – at a discrete distance, knowing he was a Muslim – with a Moroccan fellow who worked the midnight to 8am shift. It is not easy being a Muslim in New York, and I felt I needed to know he had a friend of faith in the building. I knew he sent his money home to his wife and children in Morocco, and how he must miss them terribly. I would come down at 6 am for my daily runs and Abdurrahman would be there, exhausted from his night shift. A few words of encouragement were always exchanged between us: me for a good run, and he for a quick end to his shift. He always smiled when I headed out the door and loudly said, "Bismillah!"

On the first day of Ramadan in 2019, I came downstairs for my run. I asked him if he was ready for the month. I teased him that he had it easy: he normally slept all day so fasting would be calm for him. We laughed and I wished him all the best for the start of this month. I wanted him to know that there was someone in the building who could share this month with him.

Later that day, I went out to hunt for dates. Dates are the traditional food used to break fast during Ramadan, as taught by the Prophet Muhammad. To find good foreign dates (the ones from Saudi Arabia are considered the best for Ramadan) in the United States is difficult, in view of the homegrown bounty from California, but I went up to Kalustyan's Near Eastern Specialty Market on 28th Street and found some Medjool dates from Morocco. I purchased a crate of them to bring to Abdurrahman. I left them with the day doorman, with the instructions that they were perishable and to give them to Abdurrahman when he came on his shift at 8 pm. "Oh, no, he won't take

them, he is doing that religious fasting thing!" he said. I smiled, and said, "Trust me, he will take these."

The next morning, I came down for my run and there was Abdurrahman. He rushed out of his booth and thanked me with tears in his eyes. I said that I wanted him to break his fast knowing that I was with him, no matter where he was. And that the Prophet was with him, too. I, selfishly, was happy that I was able to share Ramadan in spirit with someone nearby as well.

Over the past two years I have not seen Abdurrahman – a serious bike injury to my knee and Covid-19 put an end to my morning runs. Our paths never crossed, and with all the chaos of the past year and a half in New York, I had other things to worry about.

That is, until my husband had a stroke on the last day of Ramadan 2021. I came home from the hospital the second day of Eid (or Bayram, as Turks call it), and found a huge and very expensive bouquet of orchids waiting for me. Who could have sent these to me, I wondered. I looked at the card and only one word was written: Abdurrahman.

Muslims believe that good deeds are rewarded more handsomely during Ramadan than at any other time of the year, and giving charity (zakat) is important at this time. I believe that I have never received a more meaningful gift of flowers in my life. Flowers blessed by all the lessons of Ramadan, and given deep from the heart of someone who wanted to be by my side at this difficult time. His gesture reinforced me once again with the power of Ramadan and that the reaching of hands across faiths can be seamless as we want it to be. Indeed, Ramadan is so powerful a month of blessings and sharing that it touches many spirits, Muslim or non-Muslim.

Our beloved Mevlana Rumi celebrates the "table of spirit" embracing all in this poem:

The month of fasting has come,
the emperor's banner has arrived,
withhold your hand from food,
the spirit's table has arrived.

The soul has escaped from separation
and bound nature's hands;
the heart of error is defeated,
the army of faith has won.

***

Allah var, gam yok – "With God all things are possible."

Martha Trunk is an author, historian, and translator based in New York. She writes on art, history, and interfaith issues.

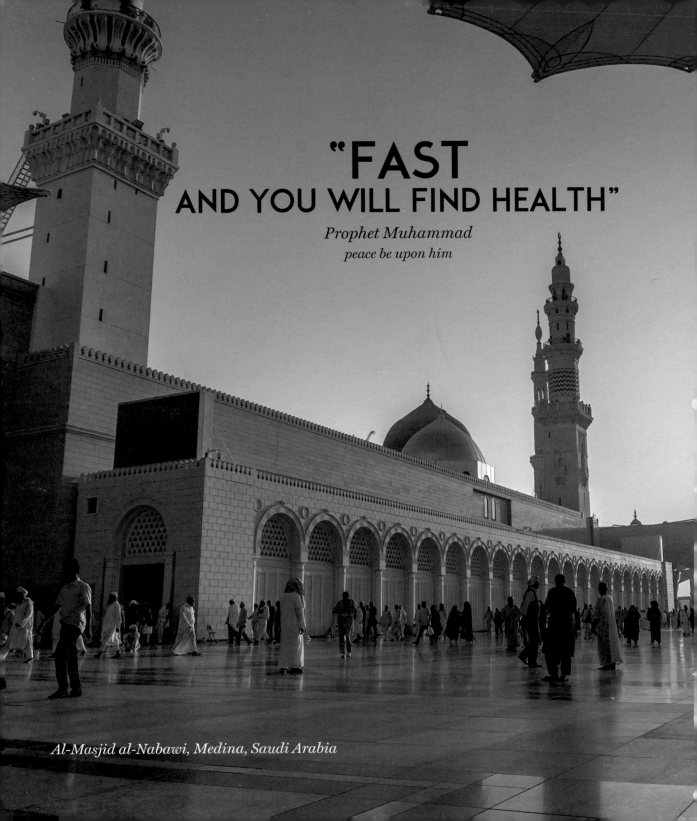

"FAST
AND YOU WILL FIND HEALTH"

Prophet Muhammad
peace be upon him

Al-Masjid al-Nabawi, Medina, Saudi Arabia